God Bless
Karl Marx!

Among C.H. Sisson's other books

Collected Poems 1943-1983
Selected Poems

Novels
Christopher Homm
An Asiatic Romance

Essays
The Avoidance of Literature
Anglican Essays
English Poetry 1910-1950

Translations
The Aeneid of Virgil
The Divine Comedy of Dante
The Poem on Nature of Lucretius
Some Tales of La Fontaine
The Regrets of Du Bellay
The Song of Roland
The Poetic Art of Horace
Catullus
Versions and Perversions of Heine

C.H. SISSON

GOD BLESS
KARL MARX !

CARCANET

Acknowledgements are due to the editors of the following publications: *Acumen, Agenda, London Magazine, New Criterion, New Poetry I* (P.E.N.), *Partisan Review, Poetry Durham, PN Review, Poetry Now, Rialto, Scotsman, Spectator, South-West Review, Times Literary Supplement* and *Westwords.* Also to the B.B.C.

First published in 1987 by
Carcanet Press Limited
208-212 Corn Exchange Buildings
Manchester M4 3BQ
and 198 Sixth Avenue
New York, NY 10013

British Library Cataloguing in Publication Data

Sisson, C.H.
  God bless Karl Marx!
  I. Title
  821'.914   PR6037.I78

  ISBN 0-85635-710-3

The publisher acknowledges financial assistance from
the Arts Council of Great Britain.

Typeset in 10pt Palatino by Bryan Williamson, Manchester
Printed in England by SRP Ltd., Exeter

Contents

Read me or not: I am nobody
For myself as for others, and so true:
If only it were also so with you
Every accommodation would be easy.
But so it is not, for what we see
Assumes as we look the mask of who,
Doing convincingly what others do:
So you become yourself without falsity.
Or so it seems. But when delusion stirs
It dreams of a mask, of his or hers,
And so must you. Where is the truth in that?
And you who read me read nothing or, worse,
What you make out for yourself, some borrowed features.
Who is what you say but I answer, what?

Vigil and Ode for St George's Day

Déjà il ne cherchait plus le bonheur
RENÉ BÉHAINE

What is the cure for the disease
Of consciousness? The cures are three,
Sex, sleep and death – two temporary
And only one that's sure to please.

In sex the circles of the mind
Close to a point and disappear
And that is something, till we hear
The world again and are not blind.

Sleep closes round us from without
Until it has us in its grip
And then the pincers start to nip:
It tells us what to dream about.

And death? Then all is gone, or so
There is best reason to believe.
In manus tuas: what we leave
Is certain, and enough to know.

For we are stone, or so they say
And how should we have ears to hear
Any objection, we who are
The treaders of the obvious way?

Either the truth is what we see
Or else it is not to be seen.
No more is it, perhaps; that green
Is grass, that tall thing is a tree.

But what else is it cunning men
Invite the suckers to believe?
All manner of follies weave
Their ways past us with if and when.

7

Yet there is truth which we assert
And I myself would die for one
If there were need, as there is none:
Better the world should be inert.

There is a time, it is enough
To know, there have been, will be times
And places when and where the crimes
Habitual to mankind, grow rough.

But we can rest in comfort, no
Mind need assert what all betray.
We in the light of common day
Without concern watch the light go.

So must it be, that only death
Relieves us at the sentry-box;
The guard comes marching up, the flocks
Of augurs' birds catch at our breath.

I watched them once, when harmlessly
They flew as martins near the house,
Dipping and soaring, and could rouse
No trouble but in memory.

A line of sceptical recruits,
Myself among them, waited for
What fortunes there might be in war
But no-one found the one that suits

Because no fate is suitable
To any man who hopes for more
Than comes his way, or comes before
He has decided it is well.

For fortune like the birds that fly
Takes its direction from the wind
Which no man changes or holds pinned
And which blows on us till we die.

The first, the bitter lot of all,
Is to be born, for so it is
As time and place and parents please
Or rather, as their fortunes fall.

Then come the choices: none is right
For none is as the birds allow;
By Aldebaran and the Plough
They pass, we into darker night.

That much is tolerable, but that
The same should swallow up our land
May not be borne, and yet the hand
Points to the hour that we are at.

The time that bore us runs away,
The place must follow, the extreme
Edge of the world is here, the dream
Breaks on another homely day.

The strong will always be unjust,
The weak will cringe and run away
Or find their comfort in a day
When they will do as all men must:

And who would dare to boast of that?
We who survive, though not for long,
May envy those who do most wrong
Yet soon enough they too fall flat.

And who is he who in the end
Loves life more than he longs for death?
Does not the most exulting breath
Turn at last to the only friend?

The spirit which was proud to be
Collected in a little earth
Finds what the privilege is worth
And in that knowledge he is free.

Fortune which holds us in its grip
Does not change, though it seems to do,
The same for me, the same for you
Whatever words are on your lips.

For what we say and what we are
Are different things, and we console
Our patience when we take a role:
Only one voice will carry far.

Christ comes to all, because belief
Is necessary for our peace,
The world cannot give it, release
Can only come by way of grief.

The Man of Sorrows is the one
Who represents the way we go:
He is the only one we know
However furious our fun.

For he knows better than the most
Experienced practitioner
Whatever comes to him and her
And that their pleasure is a Ghost.

And of death too he understands
The comfort and the mystery;
The secrets of mythology
Lie always open in his hands.

The bark of Charon and the bite
Of Cerberus, are jokes to him
Yet in his mind no single whim
The pagans have, is lost from sight

For all is laid upon the cross,
The auguries, the sacrifice,
The marching armies, every vice
And virtue, every gain and loss.

There, all was nothing to the God
Who was inside the man, who was
The man and all was all because
He died where Adam first had trod.

The intervening years were gone:
All this he did for Adam's sake
And so the future reeled to take
Another face from that time on.

The face is sorrow, like the Man,
The underworld no longer waits
To have our shadows and our fates
And where our God hung, others can.

He has gone climbing out of space
And time, yet taken with him all
That we have here, the world is small
Beside his new appointed place

Which also leaves him where he was
Before he came, but with a new
Body which he already knew
From his intent to visit us.

Our bodies too, so lifted up,
Will shine as his does, so they say,
But that is for another day
When we have also drunk the cup

Which will not pass, and when we leave
The world we credit now for one
Invisible under our sun
And in which none of us can believe.

So glory, laud and honour, all
To the impossible, and most
To Father, Son and Holy Ghost
And let our own pretensions fall.

They may, but only if we love
No other as we love our end.
The night comes down upon our friends
As on ourselves, yet still above

Their graves, the grass grows and the sun
Shines upon others as on us:
The fieldmouse and the weasel pass
And do not ask whose will is done.

But we, who saw our friends depart
Into the shadows of the moon
Leave others, as it may be soon,
Glad we are gone or, in their hearts

Holding our tiny memory
A moment till that too goes out.
Why not? For we can never doubt
The comfort of mortality.

Yet may Time's treasure still remain
Until it quietly ebbs away
Beyond our knowledge, England's day
– I cannot help it, for the pain

Of her demise is more than all
The mind can suffer for the death
Of any creature that draws breath,
And should her time come round again

Our dust will stir, not to a drum
Or any folly men devise
But to the peace which once our eyes
Met in her fields, or else in some

Of her best children, from the first.
All this is folly too and yet
Rather than any should forget
Let this sad island be immersed

In raging storm and boiling seas.
Let no man speak for her unless
He speaks too for her gentleness
And it is her he seeks to please.

Waking

May has her beauties like another month,
Even June has her pleasures. I lie here,
The insistent thrush does not trouble me
Nor the slight breeze: a tree stump looks like a cat.
Yet all is not altogether well
Because of memory; crowd round me here
Rather, you ghosts who are to drink of Lethe.
Who else would go back to the upper world
Or take again the nerve-strings of the body
Or will to suffer grief and fear again?
Once I did: and the echo still comes back,
Not from the past only – which I could bear –
But from the young who set out hopefully
To find a bitter end where they began
And evil with the face of charity.
I have seen some such and do not want
Ever to pass along that road again
Where blind beggars hold out their hands for coin
And saints spit in their palms. This I have seen
And shall see if I wake from sleeping now.

Another Waking

Was it a cat squealed or was it metal,
This grincement I heard as I awoke?
A cloud in the sky and a cat under the bed,
Both perhaps startled by my waking.
The cloud steamed forward, lumen de lumine,
A puff of white travelling over the blue.
The cat? There was an impact in the bushes,
I saw it no more than uncertainly.
Incident? Hardly. Machination, dream?
What else is there? Things are what they seem.

Cotignac Again

Cotignac is full of spies
– Not one but tells lies
Or whatever interests him;
Not one but looks out
To enquire who's about,
To mark him down and take his name.
The windows may be high, the wall
Blank, it does not matter at all:
Nothing is impervious
To the man who is callous.

Cotignac is full of thieves
– Not one but leaves
Footprints everywhere. How can
We hope to find the right man?
How believe what is said
By a man who may be dead?
How know if we are known
Or can be, by such a one?
How escape certainty
Which is of all pleasures the least?
How know what we know
When we dislike it so?

False amour where truth is found
There is none around:
The imaginary point
Puts all out of joint
– Lies, lies and lies.
So, the imaginary
Point recedes and the fact
Formerly exact
Loses reality.

Dead man, you are a lover
In the spaces of hell, either
Racketed by images
Or tendentious ghosts.

Satan in all his pride is
More complacent than most:
You mop and mow
Among the least,
Up and down, around,
Fabulously misplaced,
Erroneous, king of error,
Queen of yourself or
Mere bath-water running out:
Do you not hear the gurgle?
Follow the circle,
An ape with others, holding hands.
The supreme exit is at hand
– City of rascals, the
Infernal city
Where every inhabitant
Is imaginary.

The Absence

How can it be that you are gone from me,
Everyone in the world? Yet it is so,
The distance grows and yet I do not move.
Is it I streaming away and, if so, where?
And how do I travel from all equally
Yet not recede from where I stand pat
In the daily house or in the daily garden
Or where I travel on the motor-way?
Good-bye, good-bye all, I call out.
The answer that comes back is always fainter;
In the end those to whom one cannot speak
Cannot be heard, and that is my condition.
Soon there will be only wind and waves,
Trees talking among themselves, a chuchotement,
I there as dust, and if I do not reach
The outer shell of the world, still I may
Enter into the substance of a leaf.

Song

Others shall live instead of me
The old say, with a silly grin.
What pleasure in a withered skin!
The real life is all within.

And then the others? God, they stink,
They sweat, for they live normal lives
But when they suffer, nothing thrives,
They drink all day or beat their wives.

If others live instead of me
I'd have them do it tidily
Not bothering the old at all
– So wide is human sympathy.

What Do You Know?

Not all the reasons that they give
Will ever make their actions live.
      Reasons, ha, ha!
You think you have them when you say
Some words that you learned yesterday.
      Ha, ha!

What takes the sun across the sky?
What makes you cough or spit or sigh?
      Reasons, ha, ha?
You do what you must do, you do
What seems because it seems to you.
      Ha, ha!

Mirrors flash everywhere, before,
Behind, which makes your reasons more.
      Reasons, ha, ha!
Election, with a touch of grace,
Can save your independent face?
      Ha, ha!

Perhaps the course of history
Will turn out dialectically?
      Reasons, ha, ha!
So that's the shape it is? Ah well,
So you know that! How can you tell?
      Ha, ha!

The swindle of the world, the mind
Visited upon humankind,
      Reason, ha, ha!
You may be sure, is never sound:
Take a look at the whirling ground.
      Ha, ha!

The Description

Ne dites pas: la vie est un joyeux festin;
Ou c'est d'un esprit sot ou c'est d'une âme basse.
Surtout ne dites point: elle est malheur sans fin...

Do not describe human life at all,
Any description is a load of rubbish:
Live it – as you can not avoid doing
And therefore you can make nothing of that.

The descriptions, whether gloomy or enticing,
Are comforts of a kind, to their inventors,
But the world spreads out underneath them
Inscrutable as ever, like lands in flood.

No word covers a square inch unharmed
But what the harm is, we do not know
Nor do we know what the knowing would be
If know and harm are the right words.

No word is right, that is the long and short of it,
No saw is true, though it is nice to think so;
Even these verses wobble in the making
And yet I have brought them to an end.

The Hare

I saw a hare jump across a ditch:
It came to the edge, thought, and then went over
Five feet at least over the new-cut rhine
And then away, sideways, as if thrown
– Across the field where Gordon and I walked
Talking of apples, prices and bog-oak,
Denizens of the country, were it not
That denizens do not belong, as they do
And the hare tossing herself here and there.
And I? If I could, I would go back
To where Coombe Farm stood, as Gordon's stands
Trenched in antiquity and looking out
Over immense acres not its own
And none the worse for that. You may say
It is the sick dream of an ageing man
Looking out over a past not his own.
But I say this: it is there I belong,
Or here, where the pasture squelches underfoot
And England stirs, forever to hold my bones.
You may boast of the city, I do not say
That it is not all you say it is
But at the Last Judgment it will stand
Abject before the power of this land.

On the Prayer Book

The empty bucket, sound, clangs in the well
And draws up nothing, banged against the wall.
Was meaning down there? It is dry now
And all around the well-head chirrup and mow
Empty figures of silken Why and How.

To His Grace the Archbishop of York

with recollections of his contribution to the BBC 'Sunday' programme,
30 December, 1984

A shepherd in a northern town
Saw angels just above his head:
"They look like geese to me!" he said
And took his bow and shot one down.
"That will do, as I am a sinner
For Mrs Joseph's Christmas dinner!"

He seized the bird and dragged it round
To where the happy couple slept:
"My dears, take this." And as he stepped
Inside the stable, there he found
A baby with a brilliant future.
"It shows," he said, "in every feature.

"Why, bless my soul," he added laughing,
"Mary, they said you were a virgin!
The truth, I said, is just emerging.
By God, and here it is! A passing
Joke but I mean to keep it up
When I am made an archbishop!

"By mirrors and prevarication
I will proceed, they will like that;
The creed is rather awkward but
It works, in the imagination.
None the less I put more reliance
On stinks and elementary science.

"God, I am sure, won't touch my minster;
He only works in images,
They're harmless, aren't they? What a wheeze!
As soon suppose he'd make a spinster
Into a mum, as that he'd trade
In medals for the Fire Brigade.

"Pull up the ladder, Jack, the rungs
Are words I used in my ascent.
The Word is nothing different
And earlier ages got it wrong.
After all, Athanasius
Can hardly count as one of us!"

Thoughts on the Churchyard and the Resting-Places of the Dead

FROM THE GERMAN OF ANDREAS GRYPHIUS

for Kurt Ostberg

1

Where am I now? Is this the ground
In which humility may flower?
Is there refreshment to be found
For those who knew in busier hours
The heat and burden of the day?
And bore the frost of bitter nights
And in the midst of hurts and slights
Took up their share of care and pain?

2

Where am I? Here are the narrow plots
Which hide within their pregnant wombs
What has been sown there by the God
Who can wake corpses from their tombs.
Where some see splendour, I see fear.
Not for me the Hesperides
Or Babylonian luxuries;
I see the best of gardens here.

3

Although here no seductive scent
Streams from the jasmin and the rose,
Although no tulips here present
Their brilliant military shows,
Though here no cultivated land
Grows pomegranates or such-like fruit
It bears here what I long for but
What the world does not understand.

4

O School, in which the best instruction
Is given to us mortal men!
No pages full of false deductions
And no delusive apophthegms.
While I have passed in vanity
The wasted treasures of my time
The hours spent here instead define
The straight way to eternity.

5

O School, which utterly appals
Those whom the world regards as clever,
Which those for whom repute is all
Or money all, regard with terror.
O School which terrifies the mind
That knows the lot and has no conscience!
O School which offers no emollients
To cut-throats claiming to be kind.

6

O School, which puts men in a sweat
And makes their hair stand upon end
When they are near the judgment seat
But nearer their lascivious friends.
O School, which makes a man's knees knock
And his limbs tremble, cold as ice,
Because with all money can buy
He knows his mind is closed to God.

7

I go to school with you and long
To fathom where true wisdom lies.
Examine me! There's nothing wrong,
You will find, with my ears or eyes.
What Socrates once taught me, now
Is nothing, and the Stagirite
Has quite collapsed. There is no light
In Greek philosophy I know.

8

Who is there now that will explain
The subject that I want to master?
Set out the principles and main
Conclusions that I should hold fast to?
Or can I here and on my own
Sit down and work the answers out
That will put paid to every doubt
That troubles me? No, not alone.

9

What's happening? Is the ground I stand on
Reeling? And is that roar the trees?
Is the earth tearing its mouth open
So as to let the roots get free?
Do I hear dry bones rattling? Say,
Do I hear clamorous human voices?
Is that the south wind getting boisterous?
Or heavy stones, rolling away?

10

I stand and stare. A bitter cold
Freezes my veins, my heart, my lungs.
From my brow streams of sweat have sprung.
I am glued where the ground still holds.
The whole field has become a grave
And all the coffins are revealed.
What dust, brick, plaster once concealed
Is open now and plain as day.

11

O last but still uncertain house!
The refuge into which we creep
Whenever the clock tells the hour
And the rose pales upon our cheek.
That palace, which the world once gave,
Swearing that it would last for ever,
That same world, once our life is over
Destroys to assail us in the grave.

12

You for example were wrapped up
In tin and you perhaps in copper.
And you perhaps once had a flood
Of liquid lead to line your coffin.
You were rich, no expense was spared;
This one, now that I think of it
Had gold and marble in his pit.
Then how is it I find you bare?

13

Ah, greed and fury have not scrupled
To open up the grave's dark night,
And what I sought in pain and trouble
Lies patent in the deathly light.
Ah, lifeless men, no robber's hand
Would have intruded on your rest
Had you seen proper to entrust
Your bones in plain boards to the sand.

14

For even cedars shrink at last,
The rotten pine-boards go to nothing
And the oak's strength is quickly past,
The grave is her grave, no escaping.
Why do you value the light fir?
The joints will always crack and split.
The narrow box will go to bits
However hard you caulk and hammer.

15

God help me. Coffins open wide,
I see the bodies in them move.
The army of the once alive
Begins to exercise anew.
I find myself surrounded by
A host death has deprived of power,
A spectacle which forces showers
Of burning tears from my blank eyes.

16

O spectacle which makes the world
And what the world most values, stink.
I feel my arrogance desert me,
My courage and my folly sink.
Are these the men who ruled our land,
Defied it, knocked it, held on tight,
Who sharpened daggers, swords and pikes
And held it down with bloody hands?

17

Are these the men who mollified
The Father's heart with sighs and prayers?
Who, though distressed and mortified
Dared face his anger with their cares?
Who bewailed nothing but their faults
Though money and possessions vanished,
Though anguish left the body famished,
The oppressed spirit nipped and gnawed.

18

Are these the men who put aside
All trace of decency and shame,
Who brought from hell into the daylight
Abominations without name?
Who piled up crime on crime, who slit
Throats for fun, poisoning the world
Until the hour when they were hurled
With thunder and lightning into the pit.

19

Are these the men who were not stained
By pleasure in their pleasant youth,
Whose young minds were early inflamed
By passionate desire for truth?
Those who now sing before the Lamb
The joyful song not many know
And walk in garments white as snow
In endless peace before I AM.

20

Are these those who once strutted round
In purple, silk and gold, and these
Those who crept by on humbler ground
In hunger, nakedness, disease?
And these those whom envy so roused
They begrudged others even breath?
Whom no land could contain? In death,
In what packed quarters are they housed?

21

Where are the miracles of grace,
Beauties who captured souls by storm?
Of their delights I see no trace,
Only some ghastly heads, deformed.
Where are those whose store of knowledge
Astounded everyone? Who were
Honoured as great philosophers?
Time has demolished the whole college.

22

Now for the most part all I find
Is bones from which the flesh has slipped,
Skulls with no cover of any kind,
Faces without noses or lips,
Heads missing skin or maybe ears,
The brow and cheeks have gone to nothing
And where the lips should be hanging
Only a tooth or two appears.

23

The bones that once made up the spine
And neck, still somehow hang together
But nothing now keeps them in line,
The ribs stick out and they will never
Again hold heart and lungs close pressed;
The chest's as empty as can be,
The contents eaten, similarly
The double pleasure of the breasts.

24

What use now for the shoulder-blades?
The arms have now lost all their strength.
What served the man in all his trades,
The hand that had the management
Of tools and achieved mastery
Of sea, land, air and dared such feats
Of heroism, is in pieces,
Deprived of all activity.

25

The belly empty, hip and shin
And foot are nothing now but bones,
Hollow, misshapen, yellowy green,
Broken and dry like shards or stones.
In thousand-shaped deformities
Deformity is recognised.
Here every quality's disguised,
Young, old, poor, noble, lovely, wise.

26

And these are they against whom time
Has fully carried out its sentence;
There is no trace of flesh or slime
Mortality could take from them.
Far more repulsive are those here
Who wrestle still with putrefaction,
On whom decay pursues its action,
Those who were with us till last year.

27

The pretty ringlets fall away,
The plaits begin to come apart.
Where the moist flesh still has its say,
About the temples, movement starts.
And the unseeing eyes begin
To be unstable, as the worms
Inside the head hatch out and stir,
Wrinkle the nose and break the skin.

28

The lovely cheeks crumple and shrink,
The chin and tongue and teeth show white.
Upon the coral lips black ink
Spreads blots which put colour to flight.
The forehead splits, the snowy throat
Becomes earth-coloured, as if the sun
Which shone above it, had begun
To melt the frost and the soil showed.

29

What whisper comes out through the wind-pipe?
What is that hissing in the breasts?
It seems to me that I hear vipers
Whistling their music with the rest.
What an intolerable vapour
Rises into the frightened air
Made heavy by the poison there!
So is it by the Avernian lake.

30

So steams the marsh of Camarina,
So smoke the yellow dragons' dens.
The tortures of the Japanese
Do no worse to half-strangled men
Than the plague striking from the mist
Which rises from the popping corpses
Bathed in sweet oils not long before
And incense brought from lands far distant.

31

Filth from the guts breaks through the skin
Where the maggots have bitten through.
I see the guts dissolving in
Pus, blood and water. It makes me spew.
The mildewed flesh that time has left
Is gobbled by a snaky mob
Of bluish worms which do the job
As if they revelled in the mess.

32

What is the use of aloes now?
They cannot keep beauty in shape.
What about myrrh? It has no power
To stop the youthful limbs from ageing.
Is what came out of Palestine
Asphalt or flesh? There is no knowing.
We cannot tell, of all these bones,
Which went with which in former times.

33

What use now is a splendid dress
Embroidered with a golden thread?
And is not all this silk now pointless,
Embellishing the banished dead?
See how the purple loses colour
And all that work becomes unpicked,
How quickly patterns are unfixed
Which once cost hands so much endeavour.

34

You dead! Ah, what I learn from you!
What I am, what I shall become,
A little dust that the wind blew
Is all I carry to the tomb.
How long will my body persist?
How soon shall I conclude my years?
Say good-bye to those left here
And go where time does not exist?

35

Shall I be able to prepare
Thoughtfully for the long journey?
Or shall I have no time to spare
When I am called whence none returns?
Do not be sudden, Lord of Life,
Or send for me without warning!
But be with me on that last morning,
Protector, guide, my Way, my Light.

Where shall I leave my lifeless body,
Entrust it to the final grave?
How many, thinking to make ready,
Have their tombs built, but yet in vain!
How many lie in unknown sand?
Who can guess how chance may fall?
How many has the ocean rolled
To throw up in an unknown land?

It does not matter very much
Whether I'm married or lie alone,
Lord, so long as I may touch
Your garment, pleading at your throne.
I see the appointed hour like some
Tremendous prelude with great crashes
Of thunder and great lightning flashes,
And soon eternity will come.

When, amidst prodigies and trumpets,
We hear God's final battle-cry
Echoing through every land in triumph
Announcing death itself must die,
When marble, copper, metal, stone
And Pharaohs' tombs from their long night
Deliver to the air the light
And re-invigorated bones;

When the sea gives up its dead
Casting up thousands on the shore
From its deep gulfs and tangled weed
The bodies that the Judge has sent for,
When what the north wind blew off course,
What tigers ate up in Morocco
Or flames devoured in Persia,
What rivers that were sown with corpses;

What the Brazilian cannibals
Ate, wilder than their own wild beasts,
And those whom appetite for gold
Buried beyond hope of release;
When what Vesuvius overwhelmed
With burning ash and blazing sparks,
What Ætna buried beyond help
Or Hekla spat at in the dark;

When what time winnows in the air
Will suddenly be whole again;
Prisoners, however deep they are
In dungeons, will become free men
To see the Son of the Most High
Come in glory and put to shame
His foes, and in his Father's name
Sit where all causes will be tried.

Now hear how the Judge will pronounce
His principal and final sentence,
He who himself was judged here once
And bore it for me with all patience,
Who gives new light from heaven above:
How he makes earth dissolve, and breaks
The heavens asunder! Here stand and quake
The Jesus-haters, the Jesus-lovers.

Those whom I see here now without
Distinguishing one from the other
I shall see (as I cannot doubt)
Plunged into joy or sorrow, either
Into joy more than sense can know
Or sorrow such as none felt before,
Into delight for evermore
Or everlasting loss and sorrow.

44

Joys that the world cannot contain,
Sorrow before which Hell will reel,
Pleasure that destroys all pain,
Sorrows none here could bear to feel,
Pleasures that will drown all cries,
A sorrow that is pure despair,
Bliss which leaves no place for care,
Sorrow so keen it never dies.

45

Then I shall see you in your skins,
Free from corruption, with full veins;
All that before was hidden in
The grave, will be alive again.
I'll see you, but how different!
Transfigured some, O what delight!
Others disfigured, terrifying!
Joy! I shall shout, and then lament.

46

I'll see you shine with more brilliance
Than would be in ten thousand suns.
I'll see you and avert my glance
From those who have no consolation,
See some more beautiful than beauty,
Some uglier than ugliness,
Some finding comfort, some the darkness
Pregnant with ghosts and devilry.

47

Many the world called good and great
God's sentence designates as lost.
Many spat on and reprobate
Are chosen for the heavenly host.
Never mind how the marble reads,
Epitaphs may be pitched too high.
Corpses however cannot lie
Nor this Court ever be deceived.

48

The corpse shows that you must decline
In rottenness and stink to dust,
That nothing in the world's too fine
To go to ashes when it must,
That though we are not equal here
In death there is equality.
Go and prepare your case and be
Wide awake when the Judge appears.

49

He alone knows how to distinguish
In the confusion death has brought
Who will depart to endless anguish,
Who find the peace that they have sought.
He ensures that no single speck
Of dust from bodies shall escape him.
Air, wind and water keep from him
Nothing, in spite of time and death.

50

You dead! Ah, what I learn from you!
What I was, what I then shall be!
What is eternal, what is true!
No more the world shall trouble me.
Oh you who lie there, teach me so
To stand, that when I end my days
And take leave of the world, I may
Leave Death, and find Life where I go.

Toys

The brightness that things had, at one time!
When the curtain went up, everything was there,
Brilliant, alive, coloured. These two bricks
Recall it, but I cannot live again.

Miscellaneous Notes

1

Imitation silver and gold
Is all the money we have nowadays but since
The currency is only current and runs
Away anyhow to what it represents
Better not bother about the original metal
Which is only secondary, after all.

2

Better not go in for too much kissing,
I think nervously at one of those parties
At which old people greet one another effusively.
False marks of affection! as I would think,
Remembering kisses of another complexion
And not wishing to profane Aphrodite Anadyomene.

3

If things seem not to be as once they were
Perhaps they are as once they seemed to be.

God Bless Karl Marx!

A centre in a kingdom is absurd
You say? And where else would you find a word?
A theory, like a skein of mist that covers
The sacred members of a pair of lovers,
Mythological giants strewn by the way
Of history? The proletariat, say,
Reluctantly embraced by the middle class
Or some such dream? I at least
Prefer the ground under the two-backed beast:
Wet or fine it is less phantasmagorial,
You may even get a damp touch of the real
Or so it seems to me. Not only giants
But field-mice, rabbits, creatures more compliant
With grass and molehills – even human beings –
Shaped and sized more conveniently for doing
Whatever moles and men and women do,
Live in that terrain, having private limits
Less subject to the theoretical gimmicks
Of Marx and others living in a library.
Their words and noises are the things we see
Or hear or touch or smell, the mist that swirls
Around them is not everything in the world,
Just one delusion butting against others;
They say their piece and then their life is over.
If history rolls on they are not with it,
They understand for only half a minute
And then go blank. But the great sage Abstraction
Flies like a pterodactyl, with an action
Appropriate for imaginary millennia
Before or after there were any men here.
Here? Yes and now. Enough past for a man,
Some sunlight, moonlight, changing clouds that can
Be caught for a moment in an eye
Which must wear spectacles and then must die.

Looking at Old Note-Books

It would seem that I thought,
At that time, more than I ought;
I noted the reflections
Of those for whom perfection
Came in a sudden phrase:
How one should behave,
How others did, the wise
Remarks of men in difficulties
Or who observed others
Making a great pother
While they were easy themselves.
All this should have been useful
To a young man rising twenty,
Yet one finds that at thirty
He was still floundering.
If he understood anything
It was by way of suffering
For his first incompetence
Or third or fourth inability
To do anything sensibly.
How much had the wise helped?
They could do nothing themselves,
Being dead, buried in books
In octavo or folio, works
In several languages
And always, phrases that pleased.
What price then Schopenhauer,
Throwing a woman downstairs,
Fénelon, Proudhon,
Goethe in Eckermann
Or Plutarch in North?
I might add, "and so forth"
– Out and around
The world but all bound
In antique leather,
Mercure de France yellow
Or the elegant brown or black
Of the *Insel-Verlag*.

There was the London Library
Doing its best to confuse me
– Then back to Valéry,
Antoine de St-Exupéry,
Barrès, Cocteau, Jouhandeau
And what d'you know?
On oriental customs,
To confirm my observations
There was the Abbé Dubois
Or the Japanese school reader
For children of five.
It can cause no surprise
That with such learning
For half an hour each morning
And a supplement at night,
I knew my way all right.
The world opened before me
Like a speck in memory,
I grew in wisdom
Like a mastodon
Or other inept animal.
Behold me now, in old age,
Seated in my cage,
Pulling through the bars
What leaves can be reached from there.
Naturally I advise
The young who would be wise
To follow my example.
They should all read examples
Of the philosophers, I recommend
The moralists of course and
The epistemologists,
There is a long list.
They are not to reject
The theologians, I expect
They will find them illuminating.
Imaginative writing
Isn't all it's cracked up to be:
Take it cautiously.
Avoid writing poems, a frequent

Cause of discontent;
You may read one occasionally
And that is all
– And all I can tell
You about how to live well.

Things

It is unbuilding now,
All I have to do
– Down, down and down.
It did not matter, no.

A man should have a thought
Or so I thought
But why did I think that?
I suppose, caught

By time and place,
By a name or by a face.
Why not? For then and there
That was my case.

Things rule, O.K.? The mind
Is left behind:
Dazed and amazed, numb
Not, alas, blind.

Epitaph

His full folly he would not confess to:
He could not judge what showed his better sense;
His vices – he was reckoned to possess few –
Were, like his many virtues, a pretence.

Conclusions

★

How superficial is the mind of man!
Unhappiness, which I see everywhere,
Comes often from the thought those things are true
A momentary culture entertains,
While underneath the pull and thrust of pain
Savages those who do not understand
But have to live. Oh, how we have to live!

★★

It has gone, the old mystery
And I stand bleakly before the rain:
The church-tower sinks among trees;
Only mist remains
– Cloud fallen upon us
O let it be
Heavier than earth upon us.

★★★

All things askew: the wind
Blows from a distant forest
Composing Sibyl's leaves.

The thought is aloft, carried
Contemptuously above tree-tops
And cannot look down.

Below in the woodland path
There is moss, there are scuffed leaves.
Who walks there, rat-face?

★★★★

Now I am back in my own fen
And night has fallen, I peer through the willows
At no-one approaching across the water.
I let my past slide from me like the mist.
The ghostly people pass, of them at least,

44

Their bodies gone, only the shadows stay
Of ghosts that passed them, in other times,
Themselves made of shadows, and of what?
Ilot or island, home of the blest
Or of no squeaking figures but of the trees,
Bulrushes, sedge, from which the snipe emerge
Saying they have a thought, but they have none.
I have it. And yet I cannot grasp
Any except that their course is crooked.
So life ends without even a farewell:
Uncertainty remains the end of all.
The loved join the unloved, the violent
The gentle, even beauty is everywhere
And night falls stunningly, soon to be day.

News

They live in the excitement of the news.
Who is what? What is that? And is the noise
I hear from an important quarter? When
Is what to happen? Who is what, finally?

Finally nobody is anything,
That is the end of it, my busy friend
And just as what you hear has no beginning
It has, assuredly, no certain end.

The end that comes is not the end of what,
The end of who perhaps, and perhaps not;
The rattle and the flashing lights are over,
Death is overt, but all the rest lies hidden.

Think what you will, nothing will come of that,
What you intend is of all things the least;
As you spin on the lathe of circumstance
You are shaped, it is all the shape you have.

On a Marxist Litteratus

I expect he sees the Revolution clearly,
I expect he intends to be there early:
So much to lose, so much perhaps to win
If he is only the first man to be in.
Smart in his Russian overcoat, and with fame
Still polishing the buttons in the name
Of an imaginary working class,
He really could be the first to surface.
Is he a rock? Is he a heap of pebbles
A storm or even a tide or two could level?
Is that the sea or just a plate of mist?
What makes you think that such people exist?

Conscience

For any man whose words are sold
Will sell his conscience with his words:
The more he sells, so we are told,
The more the rascal should be heard.

It may be so, for humankind
Loves a cheat at a market-stall
Rattling his wares, although it finds
The goods are worth nothing at all.

Up the Arts!

Shall we make legends of our silly selves?
The lies invented by the semi-great,
By Yeats for example, cut no ice:
After a few years the truth shows through
And where is folly or invention then?
The folly heightened, the invention fallen,
The bright surface cracks, and underneath
The muddy water slinks away to sea
Or lurks still to be lost below the weeds.
All nature will resume her homely sway;
What grew will grow, what was invented, die.

For the Primate of All England

The Archbishop of Nothingness
Blew up a bag of wind one day
In place of a sermon, more or less,
At least, that is what people say

For he would preach at politics
As hard as some might hammer texts
And if one did not like his tricks
– Why, there was a great prelate vexed.

"I may not know," he said, "the truth
About what happens here or there
But I must give a line to Youth
Who love explosions of hot air.

"So there am I at this committee
Or speaking at that institute:
I pour out pints of verbal pity
And kill the country at the root.

"Item, I find the Church of England
Is much too narrow for my mind.
Shall my myopic eyes look inland?
No, rather at all humankind.

"The more myopic, the more distant
The objects I prefer to see;
The more I fluff, the more persistent
I like my discourses to be.

"What happens in the heart of Africa
Pre-occupies me day and night,
Yet half a glance at South America
Enables me to put them right.

"Then why is England such a muddle?
What every Christian child should know
Is, if the bishops there are fuddled
It's I who helped to make them so.

"I told the Queen they spoke a language
That anyone could understand:
Now bus-conductors talk like bishops
And there is Babel in the land!"

In the Var

1

Yes, it is certain that all is gone
With the winter weather, as on
Mountains snow is replaced by green;
Under the blue sky nothing that was
Recently apparent, remains because
Everywhere the fresh spring is seen.

All that is gone is not lost:
Water into rivers, the frost
Melted to uncover red earth
Sweating and glistening between vines
Like cloves in a ham, mathematical signs
Concealing what all is worth.

The dormant branches come too
Into leaf; over all the blue
Sky replaces the travelling grey.
All is not lost because what
Was here yesterday, now is not.
It is death that makes the new day.

2

Adam and Eve, the prime pair,
Not stript, because the air
Was always about them from the first:
The fine woman and the strong
Man they were, but not for long,
For their birth was curst

Or, not being a birth, there was a flaw
In their heredity, or else they saw
Things as they were but the presiding
Manipulator did not approve.
Be that as it may, love
Which united them, was dividing

And their mutual reproaches
Had the effect, as you may guess,
That they grew old and hideous
To one another, their bodies decayed
With the evil that made them afraid:
So much for being lustrous.

3

What is it the blue sky
And the lost darkness signify?
Nothing but the usual change.
It happens that in your case
The profound evil has taken place,
The light has gone out. Nothing strange.

For of evil there comes the good,
Not as usually understood
But different, that is all.
The new world comes, the old
Has no mind further to unfold
So that the end is fatal.

Yet not so neither for after spring
Summer infallibly comes racing,
The grapes swell and turn colour,
Autumn is here, the juice
Pours in cascades through the sluices
And then it is winter.

4

Unending, unending, or if
There is an end, the gift
Of the immutable and so
Without end or beginning.
It may be so, that is something
I do not want to know.

The horror of the world is enough,
The permanent evil, with love
Cast as the occasional good.
That this too should be permanent,
Free as it is of all intent,
Is possible. It is Christ's blood.

Credo quia impossibile
Or not at all, the light of day
Promising what it cannot perform
Or not to be credited.
Accept nothing that can be said
For to lie is normal.

5

But what of the lying light?
The shadows, under the bright
Sky the subservient Maures
Crouching between us and the sea?
The dazzle we do not see
Lapping the murderous and corrupted shore?

What of the Bessillon
Where so much murder was done?
Where were the hostages shot?
Of the dead – all the dead, for me?
It is calm now, let them be:
They are happy who are not.

Not or not, the choice
Rides over the speaking voice
Into unperceived distances.
No effort that does not creep
Under a blanket and sleeps
As the light grows less.

6

Implacable enemy, time, change,
Always the new and strange
Come to my door which is
Open to all strange visitors:
Yet, if I ask for more,
Death then to all occurrences!

– Death which is tiredness,
Neither more nor less,
The clanging angels
Are too noisy, the light
Wherever it comes from, too bright.
In change and death all is well.

To a Satirist

Leave Swift out of this;
You are paid for what you say.
Every dog has his day:
Bark like a journalist.

What you think is what they pay:
They cry "Halt" and you desist.
Leave Swift out of this;
You are paid for what you say.

The Voyage

Happy the young man who disregards
The siren who conceals herself in words,
Stopping his ears but seizing on the flesh
Which will serve his intelligence the best:
What seas must he sail on, what strange lands
Visit before he claims to understand
What song the sirens sang or other such
Matters which do not matter overmuch.
It was not so with me: I sought to find
What errors might be in a human mind
And to embrace them all, the skimpy ghosts
Who flee like shadows when we need them most.
Yet the bold sailor comes to the same port
As I who lived on charts and false reports.
Observe the wisdom that I have today!
Which others have, who had it on the way.

Ellick Farm Revisited

The design on the ground, there it is:
Ellick Farm, Gadshill Road and 468,
As it was, as I wish that it had been,
Folly in retrospection, then as now.
As I drove to the yard, past the pond,
Or where the pond should have been, the crack of shot-guns
– A clay-pigeon shoot – and there was Laurence
Coming towards me with a broken gun
Over his shoulder; but he was pretending.
I was pretending too, the old house
That was never mine, the untampered lintels,
"1689" over the door, but not William,
Not William and Mary and the Dutch bankers:
Built out of memory then, it might have been
Eighty years before, James I,
Elizabeth not far behind, older time,
Older time still with Laurence Minot crying:
"Jesu for thy five wounds,
Help us to have peace in Ingland now."

Words

What is it that we make as we obscure
Each one our sight with words?
What starts within the mind, what voice sings
Uncertainly across our doom?

The autumn mist falls: somewhere under it
Figures move, our own, silent.
We call to one another, we are many
Yet each voice is lonely.

Forgotten fathers' voices, forgotten mothers'
Speak through our own.
Is there any man who is not a cousin
And whose voice is known?

But who they are, and who we, or whether
Is settled only by a twang
Here and there, in the darkness perhaps
Among the trees.

An ocean of voices perhaps, but whose words?
Nobody owns them perhaps, they blow away
Over the flat fields to the low hills
At break of day.

Sisson's Good-Night

Goodnight, and hang me on a tree
Or lead me to the firing squad:
Say, he pretended once to be
The patriot and the friend of God.
It is not quite so bad as that,
But once I dabbled in the Creed
And England always has my love
– Two eccentricities indeed
But hardly capital offences
One would have thought, though there are those,
Certainly, whom they do not please
And the displeasure rather grows
Than lessens, in this world in which
I find myself septuagenarian:
Politics side with poor or rich
And all the Christians are Aryan.
What did I say in all that ink
I spilt in poems, in novels or
The prose in which men say they think?
What was all that effusion for?
Hard to say: if it has a meaning
The words are there, you can find out
And you will find the author leaning
To too much hope or too much doubt
– Sometimes, they say, to plain despair;
More often, I would say, observing,
Quite simply, certain things are there
And that is more or less deserving
As others think they are there too
– And that includes the dead, as well
As critics A and B, or you,
And how right you are, time will tell.

On the Edge

Now that I have come to the edge of, edge of
The grass is so thin, nothing more
The air is thin too, and the birds forget
Their augurial purposes, and fall.

So the wide sky stares back at the questioner
Blankly. "Bring what you can
Of meaning," it says, "if you want any.
Here is none."

Taxila

There is a rail-head at Havelian
– Or was, for I was there long ago –
Around it a sweet plain circled by hills:
This was my Greece, the only one I know.

It was a ghost of olives that I saw:
I had not seen the Mediterranean light
Where it falls, but I had dreamed of it.
I who had not been born woke to the sight.

Rus in urbe, urbs in the dazzling grey
– Or was it green? – green, but so grey and brown,
A spot of light in the surrounding darkness:
Taxila was the name of the town,

The heart of all I loved and could not have;
And in that limy track, as I approached,
A child with bright eyes offered a coin.
It was a bargain that was proposed.

Would I, the soldier of an alien army,
Neither the first nor last to come that way,
Purchase for rupees certain disused drachmas
Left by the army of an earlier day?

Alexander himself came down from those hills,
Over the mountains beyond them to the north
– Far lands, the boy said, but mine was farther
And longer ago still my setting forth

For my exile burned me like the sun.
I should have bought that coin, I often thought of it
After that time, and in far different places:
It would have carried me over the Styx.

I would have returned, but there is no returning.
Yet you may rise, ghosts, or I sink to you.
The world is in my hand, breathing at last
For now I know, only the past is true.

On Reflection

I sit in an unfurnished room,
Leaning my back against the wall;
A large grey sky looks in, and I
Stare back, in case the heavens should fall.

They will not: over seventy years
They have stood up and nothing now
Will bring them down, or lift me up
Further than gravity allows.

I made the journey and came here
And had my reasons on the way.
They served their turn: each step I took
Met some occasion in its day.

The long string of occasions now,
As I look back from where they led,
Appears to be so tightly strung
That no-one could discern the thread.

Juxtaposition is enough
To hold in place the days gone by,
Snug between after and before:
But how then does the future lie?

For lie it must, or not invent
A reason for the course it takes:
So the day ends in truth or sleeps
To hear no reasons when it wakes.

Et Praevalebit

When all retire within themselves,
Each to declare that what he has found
Is nothing to anybody around,
Then friendship cracks and each one salves
His stupid conscience as he may:
Or so it seems to me today.

Only a gust of social wind
Can blow a spark into a flame
And still the heat is not the same:
The former smile becomes a grin.
Old men are grinners, and they know
Enough to think it should be so.

Then: "Leave the exit door ajar,"
They think, "for I must soon escape."
Better too early than too late
For that at least because there are
No expectations of surprise,
No cures for one another's lies.

But truth is hungry, we no doubt
For it, but it also for us
And it will eat our frowsy dust
Before we know what it's about.
It's possible that that may be
The lesson of theology.

A Dedication

Better that you should forget
Everything I ever said,
Everything I did
Should be hidden,
No-one ever know
That I was so:
But I have vanity
And you must read me.